SUDDENLY THE NIGHT

Contributions to Indonesian Literature in Translation
A Lontar Publication

Yayasan Lontar, the Lontar
Foundation, is a non profit organization
whose aims are fostering greater
appreciation of Indonesian literature
and culture, supporting the work of
authors and translators of Indonesian
literature and improving the quality of
publication and distribution of
Indonesian literary works and
translations.
Suddenly the Night is Lontar's
inaugural publication and is to be
followed by other quality works of
Indonesian literatrure.

Suddenly the Night

The Poetry of Sapardi Djoko Damono

Translated by John H. McGlynn

The Lontar Foundation
Jakarta 1988

The Lontar Foundation gratefully
acknowledges the support of Mr. Ciputra
of The Jaya Raya Foundation
in making this publication possible.

Some of the poems appeared previously in Rain Spell,
a private publication of the author and translator,
Jakarta, 1986.

Designer : Prinka
Typeface : Helvetica Light, Helvetica
Printer   : P.T. Jayakarta Agung Offset
              P.T. Grafiti Pers
ISBN No. 979-8083-00-8

Contents

Introduction

Suddenly the Night is an anthology of poetry by Sapardi Djoko Damono, a highly regarded Indonesian poet who was born in 1940 in Surakarta, Central Java. Although he is a Muslim, Sapardi attended a Catholic primary school and the images that appear in his adult poems are a frequent reminder of his "Christian" past. Perhaps it is this which gives his poems their accessibility to the West.

Sapardi began to write at an early age and long before his enrollment in the Faculty of English literature at Gadjah Mada University in Yogyakarta was contributing poems to literary journals. His first collection of poems, *dukaMu Abadi* (Your eternal sorrow), appeared in 1969 and was followed by *Mata Pisau* (Blade) and *Akuarium* (Aquarium) in 1974, *Perahu Kertas* in 1983 and *Sihir Hujan* (Rain Spell) in 1984.

Sapardi is a favorite of literary critics, including A. Teeuw, the noted Dutch scholar who has overseen the development of Indonesian literature and whose books are basic texts for anyone who wishes to gain a comprehensive knowledge of the subject. With the exception of the first poem, The Three of Us, the poems in this collection are arranged in chronological order. This helps to illustrate the point which Teeuw made in his book, Modern Indonesian Literature, when he wrote: "There is a clear development discernible in Sapardi's poetry which is most apparent from the formal structure of his poems. His earlier work, including nearly all the poems in *dukaMu abadi,* posseses all the conventional characteristics of poetry: a division into stanzas and lines, and sometimes, though not regularly, rhyme and other typically poetic features. The build-up of the meaning of the poem is linked to the formal structure — which does not mean to say that a formal structure is imposed upon pre-existing ideas. Rather, the ideas, images and impulses are structured into the pattern of the various types of poem, thus developing their meaning . . . One finds tension between formal verse structure and the syntactico-semantic build-up that is so typical for modern poetry throughout this collection."

Over the years, Sapardi has let himself swing loose from the tenets of formal poetry and many of his later poems might arguably be described as prose rather than poetry; the "poetic texts" that appear towards the end of this collection have none of the constraints of form. Neither line nor stanza nor any other formal feature is present to guide and mark the development of the idea or story. The only convention left is, as Teeuw says, *"the use of the word 'poem' itself in a paradoxical and alienating sense."*

More than any other contemporary Indonesian poet, Sapardi realizes that poetry is more than convention and that convention is not necessarily a prerequisite for poetry. Through the language of his poetry and its meaning, sound and rhythm Sapardi proves himself highly capable of depicting a highly concentrated imaginative awareness of experience. Hence, even if it is difficult to find a name for his writing style, his poems are no less poetic.

John H. McGlynn
April 1988

The Three of Us

In this room, the three of us:
I, the knife and the word —
you know, the knife is only a knife when blood is on its blade
no matter if it's my blood or that of the word

Who are you

I am Adam
who ate the apple;
the Adam who suddenly aware of his existence
was startled and felt ashamed.
I am the Adam, who later understood
right and wrong, and tried to escape
from one sin to another;
the Adam who always watches himself
in suspicion,
and tries to cover his face.
I am none other than the Adam who flounders
in the net of time and space,
unsaved from reality:
paradise lost;
because of awareness and excess curiosity
about his own Existence.
I am Adam
who hears God's voice:
good bye, Adam.

One Night

he walked westward.   good-bye, solo, my home town,
he said, his head bowed
as if he were listening to the sound of his footsteps
falling, one by one.
maybe the lights are still burning for me, he thought.
foggy pictures appeared in the glow,
he almost didn't recognize himself;   he stared ahead
then drew a deep breath.
he was alone, conversing with the night,
and he imagined a ship in the middle of the sea
rebelling against silence.

silence is liquor.   there were men with women on their arms,
people standing in groups and one or two people
off to the side standing by themselves;   at times
there is indeed no other humor
a million eyes might be staring in my direction, he thought
as he walked westward, pressing close to the past.

hello, church;   hey, are you the boy
who once cried outside my door?
he remembered his friends in that church
one christmas day, all of them in new clothing
and singing;   and he went out the door.   he wanted very much
to meet jesus but his father told him:
jesus was a bastard.
he never knew whether he had ever truly loved
his father .

maybe jesus is looking for me tonight, he thought
but he's not one to make promises with anyone,
not to meet or to be met;
he hated having promises fooled with.

he walked among the crowd of people.
and thought he heard a child praying;   he had never

been taught to pray.
there were times he wanted to lose himself in prayer
but he had never learned
the opening and the closing phrase; and didn't know why.
but maybe my whole life is one long prayer,
he said to himself and seemed satisfied
with this answer of his: life is one long prayer.

that morning he had met someone, but had already forgotten
the person's name and even the person's face: he prayed
as he walked . . .
tonight he wanted to say a prayer but he knew not how to end it,
could not discover the final word.

he always felt ill and ashamed whenever he thought
of sin;   he always felt faint
when thinking of death and eternal life.
maybe god is like a school principal, he had mused
when he was in primary school. maybe it is god
who dispenses punishment, bans naughty students from school
and allows them to drift in aimlessness,
prey to the devil.
perhaps god is giving me the eye,
he thought that night;   and sees in him a person
who forever failed in his prayers.

could she have ever prayed, he asked himself
when passing a woman.   maybe she is a spray of flowers
but had she ever met jesus
or ever been kicked out of school

hello, sky, how are you tonight;
maybe the stars are blinking for me, he thought
he had once hated the sky,
in that season when planes came down
like shrieking birds and shook the earth with thunder

(and his mother had prayed
and even mentioned his name).

at times he wanted to go to the sky, at times he wanted to roam
to a far-away land;   to a cold and touching moment
he wanted to be married, to build a home.
there was a time he had felt like a dunce
when faced with a set of figures . . . and hadn't the courage
to look at himself when in the end
he could not find the key.
at times women are flowers,
but at other times transform into sets of figures
whose key remains outside ones grasp.
but he didn't have it in him
to dream of the seminary!
he was afraid to picture himself.   he wanted to escape
from the night's lights and sounds,
to release his grasp on reality
but then he witnessed: a million people praying,
refugees advancing towards god's kingdom;
sick people and inmates of jails
long lines of lunatics.
and he was startled and stopped,
the city bell was ringing, as always
a reverberant record of eternal sorrow and grief

before him a woman laughed eerily
then offered him something which he refused.
he knew not why he had refused,
maybe because her face reminded him
of a gutter or a mass of worms;
maybe because she had a leper's mouth
and gumdrop eyes
surrounded by hundreds of ants.
but he had refused her, and he gave thanks for that;
who's side is god on anyway, he muttered

he saw people walking, like himself, alone;
and men with women on their arms and groups of people together
with faces he did not know, faces he had forgotten
faces he would remember always
faces he had loved and faces he had cursed,
all one and the same.
maybe they are nodding at me, he thought,
maybe they are waving their hands at me
because of a lengthy separation
or seeing him too often: he walked westward.

hello, he nodded, to anyone,
maybe to himself;   maybe life is a long prayer,
and silence is liquor,
he felt god giving him the eye;
and he stepped up his pace.
maybe life is a prayer . . .
maybe silence is . . . .
maybe god is watching him walking westward.

At the Grave

tiny bells raise a clamor
behind the bars of my soul;   good-bye, I say.
how can a person leave without even the wave of a hand
on the start of a very good day

now you and I tomorow
I tomorrow and now you;
tiny bells ringing clearly, a sign that we once loved,
behind the bars of my heart.   good-bye

Bell in the Rain

We hear the sound of a bell
slipping through the raindrops; perhaps coming
from the tower downtown.
And you ask: who is it that pulls the rope
that causes even the panes of glass to shake
in the deep of the night,
in the house within ourselves?

I kiss your forehead: it might be a fracas
possibly a row, the first sign
of destruction of the best of the buildings
within ourselves;
oh, we might have to leave
as prey, as victims.

Close your eyes, don't be afraid
the bell might well be the beginning of light
that vanquishes black shadows and darkened corners
in the cities and the canyons
within ourselves.
We must hold on to that belief!

Prologue

even now it is heard
Your eternal sorrow. For a moment night was suspended
as the cold fell silent, outside
the sky became a lambant haze

I faithfully recite all that has come to pass
since crossing the field of Cain and Golgotha
after secreting a thousand words, here
in these confining spaces

I greet Your suffering, that of old
which gave breath to space and time
and came to form the Word.   Which read:
the loneliness of man, ashes

The Moment Before Departure

why do we still speak
the coming darkness
hides a thousand words among the flowers
in the ever more illusory space, a perfect earth

and no one has time to ask
why the season so suddenly faded
where we are.   Remaining here alone
while outside the funeral procession waits

Walking Behind the Body

walking behind the body the wind subsides
hours blink
how unexpectedly quick
day has evanesced, broadening earth's roads

at the side: tree after tree bows its head
above: our sun, that same sun too
hours floating somewhere in between
how unexpectedly empty when breathing them in

After Accompanying the Body

is there anything left for you to ask
in regard to this?   The rain stops
as a world of never ending conversation is buried
beneath aging flowers, august days

going home with a closed umbrella in hand
children return to play on the wet road
as if in a dream horses whinny in the distant hills
perhaps we need not grow old in question

is there?   How majestic is the sky
how majestic the portal that will welcome us
all, save memories
of a cave suddenly falling silent

Pilgrimage

We edge along
the narrow path
in bare feet;   pilgrims
to the graves of those who gave us birth.
Try not to wake them!
We bring nothing.   We bring
neither incense nor flowers
only small bundles of plans
(forever postponed)
to proudly display for them.
Will we find there cruel faces,
skeletons or their bodies' remains?
No, for they are only memories.
Pine trees stabbing the sky
with roots in the hard earth.
In fact we never knew them;
our parents told us tales about them,
those ancestors of ours
but failed to mention names.
They are only our dreams
memories that make us feel
they once were.
We are pilgrims;   edging along
the end of this narrow path:
an open field
                pine trees
                        the wind
No smell of incense, no flowers;
they have been sleeping since the first century,
since that First Day.
No skeletons, no bodies'
remains.
Our parents were wise,
trapping us in lullabye tales
In our hands, a bundle of plans
above our heads
                the Sun.

Landscape

a pair of birds, rows of wire, an aging sky
day's time is almost complete, the pale twilight
awaits, and we too pale watching faithfully
for all twilights to end

Rain Falls Along the Road

rain falls along the road
a drizzle as the season slowly rustles
returning to silence once more
we gaze: the trees outside are wet again

no one turns his back. And suddenly we comprehend
the secret message
when the wind is moist and free of dust
when there is no need for haste

We Witnessed

we witnessed birds crossing the sky
we witnessed small clouds in the northern sky
when for an instant even the air fell still
for a time, for some time now we haven't recognized it

between days of sorrow and fantasy
we come to know once more
the eternal peal, a conversation without words
moments long ago vanished in man's somnolent chatter

For My Wife

look at what may come to be
look at me: before Feeling recedes
before all that remains is the sound of the trees outside
reflecting off the cave's walls

look with love.   Though silence be the only sign
when you question, in trust endure
the sky perpetuates its blue
the earth holds a spray of flowers, just for you

In Sickness

when the bell rang
conversation ebbed, as we resumed our waiting
you whispered: who else will come
who else will call to escort you to sorrow

in this room we dissolve in echoes. Outside
the night settles, forever mysterious
we faithfully begin a conversation once more
as if unending, while waiting for the bell to ring

Suddenly the Night Was Stirring

suddenly the night was stirring
a thousand Whispers
suddenly you too could wholly accept
the one and only Sorrow

Flow on, River

flow on, river, calmly to your sea
the time I stood here upright in blue
Who said: look
the air is ready. The fog could be heard descending the slope...

the time when someone forgot to wait
the news arrived and the wind suddenly floated above you,
washing away the river, a thousand words, songs and momentoes
not yet addressed to the World

A Park in the Evening

from the wings of that small bird
silence, my silence, falls
a moment arrested in a park in this city
leaves fall on the bench, as if in a dream

between arrival and eventual departure
a thousand bells peal
eternity when talking to the heart
and then to the earth.   I wait here

Someday When

Listen: we have to part.   Because
we have loved too long, because our chilren
have banished their parents
and because no house remains
still open.
At first, tears, that soon turned cold,
then we left, just as it is said in those books,
after the evening repast.
Who accompanied us?
Our own hearts, prevailing over suffering
prevailing over hopelessness, prevailing
even over silence;   they planted a citrus tree
in the garden of our former home and scratched the doorway
with lime to ward off calamity,
and then we gouged out both our own eyes
so as not to see such scenes of love,
so as not to feel the pain of remembering them.
Leaving the city we crossed the river
and felt time still flowing there
outside ourselves.   Be careful, don't look back,
there is no one there who needs us,
no one calling us back;
this affair of ours does not end here. Come along .. .

In Prayer: I

I see: Symbols in light
I see the universe
when You, in a flash, become radiant in the Word
and resound in thunder.   Beyond sound, the night is alive

the leaf clings to its branch.
as the rain begins.   I hear the earth of old
nothing stands betwen Us: the cold
glows ever brighter with the blowing wind

In Prayer: II

when even nothing did not exist
I walked   (without movement,
a possible sign)   and We met

a pair of Nothings
purified   (absent of
movement, it seemed a
pleasure):   as Silence welled

In Prayer: III

traces of Flowers everywhere; how tempting
for us to search,
to plunge into the roar of colors
before the season sheds its leaves

and later to be lost
(enticed by Flower traces)
or be caught by the shadows of Light
in our anxious passion

When the Flower Petals Opened

when the flower petals opened
we suddenly felt: the intensity
of Our love
a light like mist, a misty light; in the sky

the day's clouds skirt away; on the earth
primeval quiet thrives;
when we feel even in our eyelids, the dry season one morning
on a butterfly's wings, on wings of color

the whisper of birds on branches of light
feathers of light; how hopeless
Our love
a drunken stroll among the screams of opening flowers

Marriage Poem

Who is it, this light
(night's petals fall)
the room's horizon blurs
in Bodily Union

grain by grain
(you and I,
I and night's pollen)   fall
into one

a marriage of
nowhere and never
petal after petal opening
and night becomes perfection

Before the Final Sun

Silently you kiss the tips of your fingers.
The dry season, hissing listlessly
pierces the thin air and is thrust against you;
but that is not what you are waiting for.

Slowly you press your hands to your heart.
"How are you, Daylight;
as you did yesterday, you bring back today
the Sun's message". Then your face changes to fog

dreaming, as sleep approaches, about sleep;
as your veins begin to soften; the season has pierced them
(and at the same time placed dust
on calendar leaves). "Good afternoon,

Nature's love; for so long you were lost
together with my childhood". And later, in complete dependence
were your eyes, your spirit, your soul; suddenly a whiff,
the smell of your sweat

a sign that the entire room is waiting
for the Red Sun on the horizon to leave traces
no more: leaves in the garden, window curtains, calendar pages
dissolve in smoke. only Traces remain.

A Light Rain on Jakarta Street in Malang

it was as if you were speaking at the end of the road
(cold, the rain suddenly fell silent
as if you were calling from the corner
for a return to grief)

a return to desire
sustained and unfulfilled
as if you were signalling with no apparent sign
to anwer you, You

Two Poems With One Name

I

blood stains the plain.   Who
is the sacrificial animal this time,
from whence the silence.   How many ages have suffered
since He banished us from There

small clouds recognize him and cry:
Abel has been slain, his blood calls to the Father
(I am on your side, friend, look straight ahead
the smell of blood is still strong.
We go into the world)

II

if Your name is also Silence, let us
meet again at midday;   after I have killed
that man.   In the middle of the plain I am left alone
fending off the Sun

and You are here too.   Look at the palms of my hands
stained with the blood of my own brother
the trees stand firm, no doubt they understand
the hurt of a loyal son shunted to the side

yes.   I did kill Abel, upon whom lies
nature's heart-break, humanity's first revenge
clouds in the sky continue to pass, the wind forever
causes leaves to fall;   all in your name: Silence

I Watch the Approaching Gloom

I watch the approaching gloom
who is that over there, you suddenly ask
(at once the night turns to haze)   Perhaps he's here to meet you
perhaps to bring news of the rainy season ahead

we stand wordless at the door.   Waiting
or being waited for, with no prior arrangement
does he know you, you press   (Broken silences
rebuke us)

his shadow is almost here.   Don't say
good night; retreat slowly
(no doubt rain has already fallen
at the river's upper reaches); it is the Moment, I whisper

I kiss the tips of your fingers; you look at me
"kill him, my husband" (I stare at the gloom
whose shadow is now almost on top of me
and say: why do You stand so immobile there)

Meeting

woman sends her tears
to lands of light, to the poles of the moon
to the horizon's base: her head on the pillow
is as soft as a rainbow

man never turns back
and at each step: dense jungles
harbors in commotion;   and in his brows a pair of suns
so hard and transient

and beads of rain
approach from every direction (a veil
for the open womb, sated air)
when they meet.   In this bed

Sonnet: X

who scratches at the blue sky
who tears apart the passing clouds
who crystalizes in the fog
who nestles in the withered flower
who dissolves in the purple haze
who breathes with the pulse of time
who vanishes each time I open the door
who melts beneath my glance
who speaks in the spaces of my words
who protests in the shadows of my silence
who comes to take me on the hunt
who suddenly tears away my veil
who explodes within me
: who am I

Sonnet: Y

though we often meet
among the visitors to the grave
in the spaces of blue voices
and mires of purple and gray
though I often remember you
among words so long ago lost
and sealed in shadows
of murky desire
though I often greet you
at each change of weather
when green turns to glowing red
in the revolution of the wheel
: I know not why I yearn
  in trembling terror in the waiting room

Distance

and Adam came down to the forest
to disappear in myth
and suddenly we are here gazing
upward at the sky: empty and still . . .

Line

the black line glides
over colors of gold, in which season is it
that we must we part
not stooped with the burden of parting?

as sunlight breaks
the room fills with hoarse voices; is it you
in the dust of the rainbow
the fog inside myself?

and sharp lines (repeating
again and again are once again
turned back) on a background of gold
a sign that I am pregnant.   You leave.

Rain in Composition, 1

"What do you discern from the sound of the rain, the wet leaves of the bougainvillea slapping repeatedly against the window pane? What do you discern from the smell of the earth, from the sound of water running through the gutter?" He envisioned a mysterious bond between the earth and the rain, envisioned the secret of wet leaves and their repeated slapping.

"There is nothing save your own shadows behind the door dreaming of that slapping, dreaming of the welcome at rain's edge, dreaming of the hiss of water drops sliding from the leaves near the window. Or dreaming of a kind of syllable that might accompany you to sleep."

Most likely he has heard it too often and now no longer recognizes it.

Rain in Composition, 2

What do we hope for from the rain?   At first it's high in the
    sky, light and free; then crystalizes in cold and catching
    whiff of the smell of earth, falls and strikes the guava
    tree and sliding from its leaves, bounces off the roof
    tiles to spill onto the garden and return to earth.
What do we hope for?   The rain also falls on the long road,
    follows it, and slipping slides into the gutter rippling
    since early evening and rippling now in this dark night,
    talking about the sea.
What? Maybe there is rain that falls on the sea as well. Good
    night.

Rain in Composition, 3

and finally we sense the tick tock of the clock:
distinct from the rain

After a Brief Conversation

after a brief conversation,
colors withdrew
into white. And nature outside
awaits in vain

Morning

when the morning wind came we were suddenly nowhere
to be found.   Where is the reverberation
of our love's shadow
which even the night before was caught in surmise

among the tables, chairs and windows?   The room
mists each moment we are there
the hours are silent
until we are suddenly gone.   When the morning wind came

there was no "Where are we?"
each of us began to roam once more
in love following footsteps of Love
whose question within us is never ending

As I Wait for You

As I wait for you, kapok blooms harden
with the the peak of this barren dry season
a few junes only which I carefully noted,
but silently let go, bloomed and wilted inside me

small clouds pass over the bridge as I wait for you
seasons condense amid my lashes
I hear the repeated sound of air waves breaking
passion and lust is naked here, the stars are restless

thin dry seasons have fallen: something suddenly falls silent
among the clamor of the kapok and frangipani flowers
    as I wait for you
ever more rarely the clouds pass by
for nothing have I ever waited so long; you're not even there

Outside the Door

outside the door: shadows of moonlight
rest in the grass. Light's sudden emergence
begs them to go
to stretch out the distance with silence

The Room

when entering the room
she recognized me for sure,
my footsteps, my breathing
the tips of my fingers that once had touched her

and this time — this meeting
with no clock on the wall
so matter of fact one evening
when conversation was no longer a necessity

without quick gasps
without "how fast the night has gone!"
I saw her lips freeze
searing my memory

That Night We Were There

"why did you bring me here?"; a station
at night's end. White images at the platform's edge
stretch out upon the benches; the clock's hands, leaping
untiringly cling fast to Silence. Maybe.

we await the train that usually arrives
whenever there is no one to give the signal,
or maybe we just want to be here
when there are no people hurrying about or waiting
    in disappointment

our sighs alone, following the ties, suddenly harden;
flashing signals, yellow lamps receding in midair;
as white images fill the room: "But tell me first,
why did you bring me here?"

Japanese Garden, Honolulu

is this peace? A small glen:
a winding footpath, the sun
resting beneath the flowers,
rippling water postponing
each and every answer

On The Chicago Subway

"What is your name?" I was probably half asleep when I asked
   that again.   Half of the seats empty, faces like knives
   before me and at the window: silhouettes on a black background.   I didn't even answer you, even when you asked the
   time of my death, because when I was completely awake, you
   weren't even there.

Alright, today we'll just call it fear, or whatever. But at one time
   it may have been a hero's spoils, a slave or even
   a teacher teaching children to sing — but which beats
   faster, the human heart or the watch   (that always counts
   your intakes of breath)   when you imagine a pistol pointed
   in your direction?   Maybe we shouldn't call it anything at
   all;   you're busy repeating the same questions and I am only
   half awake.

Supposing . . .

New York, 1971

Memorize your name well here.   After the steel
and cement order our steps, the lights
and glass.   The sky is only in our hearts,
stored faithfully in the valleys where you and I
were born, growing bluer in its thirst.
Memorize your name.   Corner by corner,
color after color of traffic signs that point
in our direction and later assure
confused directions
to places once existing in our childhood dreams.
Walk close to the wall
repeating the name of the place
and date of your birth all the way to corner
of the street that goes in all directions
while at once renouncing direction.
With the growing number of people
comes the feeling of being
completely alone.   Be ready
with the answers.
But can you hear the voices?

Don't Tell Me

chapped lips of flowers
chewing on the sun,
don't tell me about cold
screaming deep in the night
— becoming dew

Writing on a Tombstone

please scatter above me life's cooler shadows
should you make a pilgrimage here
this grave is too much to endure, gasping
beneath the blazing sun

Blade

the knife's blade watches you, unblinking;
and you who have just finished honing it
think: it is sharp enough to split the apple
now sitting on the table
after your evening meal;
it shimmers with the reflection of your vein

About the Sun

That sun above your head is
the gas balloon that escaped your fingers
when you were small, the light bulb
above the table where you answer letters
regularly received from a certain Address,
an alarm clock ringing
when you make love, the picture of the moon
the child points at and says:
"It's the sun, it's the sun!" —
The sun? Yes, it's up there
so that forever you will drag behind
your shadows.

Poem in Three Parts

I

Is it cold this night
that I return to you
in its entirety?   Colors suddenly disappear
into White.   A sigh remains.

II

Behind the whispers of the bamboo grove, in tatters I await
or so you say; · aha! your enticement to kill myself is a sham
     this time too

III

the shimmering stars have made me drunk,
     with constant mention of your name
the bitter wind has made me drunk,
     with constant mention of your name
the smell of the wild grass has made me drunk,
     with constant mention of your name
I have wanted to kill you for some time now
     to become everlasting in you

Childhood Notes, 1

He peered inside the empty well and could see broken lines and shards the color of silver and black crystal he once had seen when he was sick and talking in his sleep and crying for his mother. They said there was a snake at the bottom. He threw a stone into the empty well and heard a sound that he had known long before hearing his own cries for the first time. They said there was never water in that empty well.

He tried to guess why his mother never believed them.

Childhood Notes, 2

He took a short cut and the sharp blades of grass fell beneath his feet. The sky was still the same. He imagined the sea and the flowers with jaws and thought about whether the bird startled from its branch had ever seen sea jaws or flower jaws racing for an attack. The sky was still the same. The wind was so light and could soar wherever it wished and tease the sea after teasing the flowers but he was not the wind and was disappointed and kicked a piece of gravel. There was a cry from behind the bush. He didn't hear a sound. There was a cry behind the bush and its echo touched a sprig of flowers and was caught by the wind and taken away to the sea but he didn't hear it and he imagined the jaws of the sky when it's about to rain. He arrived at the riverbank but those who had promised to meet him were not there. The sky had changed. He watched the ever-moving blackbird and those who had promised to take him across the river had still not arrived and he saw raindrops begin to fall on the water and he watched the circles widen and imagined them suddenly surrounding him and throwing him into the water.

There was someone watching from across the river but he could not see him. There was.

Childhood Notes, 3

He gets out of bed and tiptoes over to open the window and stares at the stars asking what in the world is beyond the universe and continues to watch for he feels that someone will come by to explain it all for him and he continues to repeat his questions until finally hearing the cock crow three times and when turning around sees his mother behind him telling him "let me close the window for you after staying awake all night you must go to bed because the night air is not at all good for you".

Walking Westward in the Morning

walking westward in the morning the sun follows from behind
I walk following my drawn out shadow before me
the sun and I don't argue about which one of us creates the
    shadows
the shadow and I don't argue about which of us must lead the way

Nocturne

I let the starlight possess you
I let the pale and ever-restless wind
that suddenly changed into a sign, take you from me
I know not when I might have you

The Sun Slips Away

I.

the sun slips away. When the air suddenly condensed
"Who taught you to stare at me like that?"

II.

when the air thickened and we groped in misunderstanding
there came again: the voices that banished us

That Day

We were still waiting when the wind carried in the murmur of
  the waves;
  we imagined open coral blossoms welcoming the tips of the waves
  whose spray obscured the horizon.
"He's still not here," you said; and the sound resounded off
  the wall to fade in the cold.
When we heard footsteps outside we were still hopeful; we
  imagined that the harbinger had succeeded in crossing the ocean and
  would soon announce our release.
But time always passes so quickly before the first word
  echoes, who knows what can diminish the cold that has almost
  crystalized in our veins.

Quatrain

through the night the sighs of your chest climbed the wall and
    fell one by one to the floor
in the morning you awoke to catch a whiff of a smell that
    reminded you of something no longer your own
you opened the window:
the sunlight jumped in and you could see indistinct shapes
    rising, one by one from off the floor, and transforming
    into a kind of gas though still you could hear the sound
    of sighs climbing the shafts of light

Poem, 1

So it was we talked the night long: warming ourself on
    syllables that rubbing together would burst into flames.
    "Say something, the rain that confines us will put us to
    sleep and blanket us with a long white cloth and lock the
    door to this room!"

And yes, so we did speak the whole night long: "But each word
    so quickly became ashes and scattered by the wind made the
    air all the more stifling and . . ."

Poem, 2

I folded the lakes and rivers and tucked them back into my
vein.   The forest lay bare.   Thus it was the herds of deer would
no longer live in my poems for their words were now tipped
with arrows dispatched by Rama.

Thus it was the birds could no longer nest between my
sentences for they were now so tight there was no space to
spare.   Only a few hunters remained separated from their dogs
following tracks of blood, turning over and shoving around
each letter of my words, looking for the fallen animal who had
taken an arrow in its vein.

Rainy Night Conversation

Rain, the one with the mackintosh, galoshes and umbrella
stands beside the electric pole.

It says to the street lamp: "Close your eyes and sleep. I'll
stay up tonight."

"Rain, you really do like absolute darkness, mystery and
rustling sounds: you come from the ocean, sky and earth:
return there, don't try to make me sleep.   I am man's friend
and he likes light."

Egg

An egg sits in the exact center of your neat whitebed. Coming
    home late at night you are of course startled to find it there.
    That egg could very well be one that was here and gone and here again
    in the hands of the magician you watched that evening.

It could be that your little girl or your wife or your mother
    put it there intentionaly for you to sleep peacefully inside.

I Hold Tightly

I hold the spray of flowers tightly
my husband, when the children attack.   Who knows
after they are calm
it may still be in my hand, for you

A Pair of Old Shoes

a dusty old pair of shoes lay sprawled in the corner of a
　　　storeroom
the left one thought back on softened asphalt, the right one a
　　　muddy road after the rain — both had fallen in love with
　　　that pair of feet
the left one assumed that in the morning they would be taken
　　　off to the rubbish pile and burnt along with a bundle of
　　　love letters, the right one thought that they would be
　　　thrown on the garbage truck and dumped out and left to rot
　　　with food scrapings
an old pair of shoes lay whispering about something only the
　　　two of them could understand

After the Sound of the Thunder

after the sound of the thunder I could see only
your naked body, your loosened hair floating atop
the clear and smoothly flowing water
you didn't answer my call

River in Tabanan

we stop and gaze toward the river
where women sow seeds of fog upon the surface of the river
    whose rippling can be heard from afar
we cry out "what is the river's name?" but only their peals
    of laughter come back in reply
and when arriving at the river's edge the women are not
    really there — and fog covers the river's surface and we
    don't even know if it's flowing to the north or to the south

For I Gusti Ngurah Bagus

the gods created rice
the gods created flowers
the gods created the girl with sheaves of rice on her head
    and a flower behind her ear
the gods will one day stand at the temple gate to goad the
    woman as she passes by — "old woman, stack your sheaves
    of rice in the granary and throw your flower in the
    river; allow us to instruct the people to build a fire on
    open ground and burn your body to ash

Light Bulb

A hanging light bulb glows in the room. The man knitting his
fingers together makes shadows on the wall: "It's a deer,"
he says. "Hooray," the children scream, "now make a
tiger!"

"It's a tiger." Hooray! "It's an elephant, a deer, a wild pig,
a monkey . . ."

The light bulb would like to close its eyes. It feels as if
it's in the middle of the jungle and is dizzy from the din
and the commotion of herds of wild animals. It suddenly
feels distant and ignored.

Conversation in a Room

The cigarette butt and chair talk about the man who suddenly
   takes a deep breath and stands
The plastic flowers and the wall painting talk about the man
   who stands as if trying to hold out against something
   that will destroy him
The wall clock and calendar talk about the man who suddenly opens the
   door and hurriedly leaves, not closing it again.
The mask on the wall, so like the face of its maker, hasn't
   the courage to utter a single word; it senses the man's shadow, still
   moving from wall to wall; trying not to speak, it resembles its maker all
   the more.

One Morning

And so one morning he wanted very much to cry while walking head down through the alley. That morning he wanted the rain drip-dripping down and the alley still so that he could walk alone while crying and have no one ask why.

He didn't want to scream or cry out wildly or break windows or burn the bed. He wanted only to weep softly while walking alone in the drip-dripping rain in the quiet alley that morning.

Performance, 1

a stage light burns; having forgotten to turn it off, the
    watchman is asleep,
six hundred empty seats watch a silence more powerful than
    the bat's shriek
the microphones that hang on the stage appear to be
    listening to words that the shouting prisoners dared not
    speak: "Is my performance as the silent jail keeper a
    convincing one, My Lord?"
the voices seem to grow louder —

Performance, 2

At first there was an old man on the stage in a rocking
  chair. There was a table, a chair, a cold cup of coffee,
  a hanging lamp and letters scattered on the floor. The
  old man rocked back and forth.
While rocking the man curses names we do not know and
  rebukes the table, chairs and letters — we laugh.
He suddenly stands and exits — from offstage he calls out
  names that find no reply. The chair continues to rock.
  But why do we still laugh?
Even as his voice grows hoarse and the light begins to dim
  — the chair continues to rock. We, the audience, must go
  home before we laugh again.

Performance, 3

a red spot for the bed, a muted green for the pistol hanging
    on the wall and of course a blue spot directly on the
    face of the lead
all right, a white spot for the old woman dressed entirely
    in white who unceasingly circles the stage
the black spot is of course for you — it searches for you
    among the audience now dazed from this play
my job is a simple one: when hearing your sudden scream I —
    the lighting man — must throw up all the lights in the
    house because I have already found you — for that is the
    director's orders

Water Color Poem for Rizki

the wind whispers to the fallen leaf hanging from the
telephone line, "I want you, I want to play with you!"
the telephone line reminds the wind whose anxious fingers
are clutching at the fallen leaf, "stop whispering, you'll
bother the rain!"
the rain spits at the end of the alley and with its sharp
stare scolds: "let that leaf alone!"

The Incident This Morning

for GM

This morning a jimney driver told an office boy about a man
who was hit by a cycle when crossing the street.
This afternoon the office boy told a vendor about your
friend who was hit by a cycle when crossing the street,
thrown to the asphalt and carried by passersby to the
side of the street.
This evening the vendor told you that I had been struck by a
cycle when crossing the street, thrown to the asphalt,
carried by passersby to the side of the street, had
waited a half hour before the ambulance finally came and
died upon arrival at the hospital.
Tonight you look forward to telling me about the incident
this morning.

Three Postcards

1

the problem is you were never really firm in explaining to
    Me your true position, never really admitted that you had
    yet to settle your business with Me
I've no idea where your previous letter is for it's not
    among the stars or in the cracks of clouds or the folds
    of angels' wings.
I remember it all so well: you writing My address with such
    haste — I imagine your fingers quivering — a sign that
    there was something you wanted to convey to Me as soon as
    possible

2

Where are you now? give it to me straight: did you ever
    write that letter? did a chill ever shoot through your
    body when you saw My shadows left behind in your room?
maybe I was wrong and maybe you never did feel the need to
    maintain a relationship with Me or recall the lengthy
    conversation that we had about the mask on the wall.
whatever the case, I want to know where you are

3

the kid of yours that's still at home wrote a letter which
    said, "I found Your address in the trash can, among the
    letters that father threw out; he only once mentioned
    Your name and that was the time I screamed when he
    wouldn't let me put on the mask . . ."
he must have wanted Me to tell him about why I gave you that
    mask as a gift on your birthday that year
his tactic is the same as yours: staring sharply while
    accusing that My let-there-be is an utter waste

I Stopped the Rain

I stopped the rain. Now the sun
in longing for me, slowly lifts the morning mist —
something beats
inside myself:
                piercing wet earth;
a longing made pregnant by rain
and sunlight

I could not stop the sun
from forcing me to create flowers.

Lyric for Jazz Improvization

"my far away lover:
                  how many times
have I circled this park;
rolled in the grass, bits of paper,
dew and shards of glass;
have I wrapped myself in starlight
and the wind's long sigh;   I have never slept
while waiting for you.
The old man who often passes, who spits
and always asks the time maintains
that you always keep your promises;
but the stray cur with the drooping eyes
never responds
to my whistle!"

It seems to him that he's tracing a circle
and will never find a bench.

Lyrics for a Pop Song

don't shut your eyes: I wish to remain in the raining jungle
        — your gaze is the cry of a raindrop slipping from the
        thorn of a rose   (how shrill!);   your voice, the flick of a
        falling bird's feather   (how quiet!)
I too will slowly break and dissolve in the jungle;   shining
        pollen in the haze — your breath is the waving of the
        jungle orchid about to bloom   (how sharp!)
I will dissolve in the drizzle in the raindrop in the flick
        of the bird's feather in the waving of the orchid — when
        the jungle suddenly fades
don't shut your eyes:

Mirror, 1

the mirror never screams;   it also never
moans or sobs or weeps
even though what happens is just the reverse inside it;
maybe it only can ask
why do you appear to have lost your voice?

Mirror, 2

you suddenly dissolve in the room, searching in the mirror;
but the mirror clouds when you go wherever you go
    when you condense and cling to the glass, when you suddenly
    turn to water and spatter all around;
while in vain the mirror tries to capture you

I am the Lake

I am the lake: sail upon me;
sail, stirring curls that move the lotus blooms;
sail, gazing at the fragrance of light;
sail across and leave the boat behind, without a second thought —
    I will watch it for you

Paper Boat

When you were a child you made a paper boat and sailed it at
    the river's edge; the current, so smooth, your boat weaved its way
    towards the ocean.
"It will stop at great ports," an old man said.
    And going home, you were happy, with multicolored scenes in your
    head.
    Since that time you have waited just in case news should
    come of boat that your longing never released.
And finally you hear Noah, the old man say: " I used your boat in a great
    flood and now it lies stranded on a mountain."

The Way to Kill a Bird

how does one kill a bird that crows with the chimes of a clock
    that was there on the wall even before we were born?
the problem is, it's not a bird that warbles in the morning
    and races from one sunbeam to another in the spaces of
    guava tree branches   (an entire world in window frames!)
the problem is, it calls to me at night even though it is then
    I often prefer to be alone
the problem is, it is everlasting

In the Hands of Children

In the hands of children, paper becomes Sinbad's ship
undefeated by the waves, a bird
whose cries open flower blooms in the forest;
in the mouths of children, words become the Holy Book.

"Hey, Mister, leave this game of mine alone."

Flower, 1

(i)

And even the wild flower lied.   It bloomed at the edge of the
 plain as the morning's quiet rose; in the afternoon the sky
 pulsed as a clutch of crows appeared and circled above the
 plain;   at night it heard the jackal's cry.
But it said, "Afraid?   That word is for your use alone, you
 human beings.   I am the wild flower, the gods' beloved!"

(ii)

And even the wild flower lied.   It sprouted one morning in the
 gaping maws of a stone in an old cave and at night realized
 that nothing whatsoever was visible in the cave and that
 the air was incredibly heavy and pregnant with the smell of
 a body's remains and heard what sounded like a stifled
 bleat and imagined the forest in flames and after the fire . . .

It screamed, "That is only how it looks to you, you human
 beings!   I am the wild flower, the gods' beloved!"

Flower, 2

the rose leaned away and almost said don't when the owner
of the garden picked it that day;   there was in fact no reason
to say don't because the woman could not of course comprehend
its sign — there was no reason to know why the face of the
woman who had so faithfully watered it and looked on it with
loving eyes seemed now so haughty and cold as she stripped the
petals of the bloom one by one and let them fall to become
delicate circles on the surface of the pool below

Flower, 3

the garland of jasmine flowers on the bed had turned to rust
    before it smelled the morning air and heard the knock on
    the door
there was no response
the jasmine garland was dry: its scent hanging in the four
    directions crystalized in the air when the sound of someone
    forcing open the door was heard
there came then a sound like thunder came "Hey! Who was it
    that took my body away?"

The Flute

The bamboo flute imagines that someone is playing it,
    covering and uncovering its holes, creating princes and
    princesses of unimagined beauty from far and distant lands . . .
And it searches its forever gaping holes

On a Stone

he sits on a stone and throws bits of rocks to the middle of
    the river
he plays with his feet causing the water to ripple here and
    there
he looks around him: the sun that had disappeared — appears
    in the trembling interstices of leaves, on the footpath
    winding its way up the riverbank, on dragonflies —
he so wants to believe that he is really there

Meditation

Do not disturb: I, the warrior-hermit, am meditating in a cave, an
egg or a word — is there in fact a difference? And at some
point in time when roots have encircled me, and I, a seed,
have found meaning — will you, my friend, have the courage
to approach?

Metamorphosis

something is taking your clothing off, one piece after
    another, seating you before the mirror and making you ask
    "whose body is this that I have on?"
something is silently writing your life story, weighing the
    date of your birth, seeking the cause of your death —
something is silently changing into you

Ear

"Come into my ear," he urged.
        This is crazy:
he was being tempted to enter his own ear
in order to hear anything
and everything — each word, each letter
even the explosives and fricatives that create sound.
         "Come in," he urged.
It's crazy! Just to be able to best understand
whatever it was he whispered
to himself.

Mister

It's Mister God, is it not? A moment, please,
I'm out.

Rain Spell

Rain knows well the tree, the road
the gutter too — their voices can be distinguished;
you can hear them too even when you close the door
and window.   Even when you dim the light.

Rain, who really can distinguish
has fallen on the tree, the road and the gutter —
casting a spell so that you have no chance at all
to protest when you find the revelation you may not reveal

Time is Transient

Time is transient.   We are eternal:
plucking seconds, one by one, arranging them like flowers
until one day we forget what for.
                         "But time is transient,
is it not?" you ask.   We are eternal.

Mask

for Danarto

1

He enjoyed making masks.
and would peel off his faces,
one after another and hang them on the wall.
"I like playing with them," the director said.

At night, as the play was being staged,
he sought his face among the wheezing,
shouting and complaining masks
but it wasn't there. It seemed he had more faces

to peel away, one after another.

2

"Where is my mask?" he asked to no one
in particular. In the changing room: a broken mirror,
rouge and powder in disarray;
but no mask. "Where

is my mask?" he asked. Low-watt bulbs,
cobwebs on the ceiling,
and a tranquilizer in his palm. But the mask
was not there. Perhaps the director had meant: The Tyrant

must create a mask from his own face.

3

But a mask may not become human;
a mask must follow the king's orders,
obey the commander's rules, knowing all too well
the eyes of the audience and the beating

of their hearts. Oh, dear God,
to never be listed in the play bill or receive a wage
just to be hung from the wall when the play is over.
Even when only the two of them remain behind the empty stage
the director pays no heed.

The mask has no right to become human.

Sources

Basis, No. 4, 1966

Horison, No. 5, 1968

Horison, No. 6, 1970

Horison, No. 9, 1987

Jassin, H.B. *Angkatan '66, Prosa dan Puisi* (Vol. I) (Jakarta, Gunung Agung, 1983)

Puisi ASEAN 1978 (Vol. I), stencil, (Jakarta, Jakarta Arts Council, 1978)

Sapardi Djoko Damono, *dukaMu abadi. Sadjak-sadjak 1967-1968* (1st ed., Bandung, 1969)

Sapardi Djoko Damono, *Akuarium. Sajak-sajak 1972-1973* (Jakarta, 1974)

Sapardi Djoko Damono, *Mata Pisau. Sajak-sajak 1969-1971* (Jakarta, 1974)

Sapardi Djoko Damono, *Perahu Kertas* (Jakarta, Balai Pustaka, 1983)

Sapardi Djoko Damono, *Sihir Hujan* (Kuala Lumpur, Dewan Bahasa dan Pustaka, 1984)

Sapardi Djoko Damono, Water Color Poems, translated by John H. McGlynn (Jakarta, 1986)

Sastra, No. 7, 1961

Teeuw, A., Modern Indonesian Literature (Vol. II) (The Hague, Martinus Nijhoff, 1979)